- Successful Dating -

No More Frogs
Sagittarius

22 November – 21 December

by
Cathrine Dahl

CONTENTS

Page 1 | **PREFACE: A few words about compatibility** and why traditional compatibility guides can give you the wrong idea

- Successful Dating -
No More Frogs

by Cathrine Dahl

No More Frogs - Successful Dating is your one-stop dating guide. No unnecessary blah-blah. The information is right here, at your fingertips.

This guide can be used in several ways. It's a handy tool when you want to prepare yourself a little. It can give you an advantage when going on a date or getting to know someone you've just met - or even someone you've known for a while.

Although this guide can help you angle your approach, remember to be true to yourself. Have fun, be wise, follow your heart - and keep your feet on the ground!

- Cathrine Dahl

Preface:
A few words about compatibility, and why compatibility guides can give you the wrong idea.

So you've met this Gemini you really, really like, but you're a Scorpio, and the compatibility guides say you're a lousy match. Guess what? That's rubbish!

Some compatibility guides offer a very simplistic approach, claiming that your best matches are the star signs within the same element as you:

Fire: Aries, Leo and Sagittarius
Earth: Taurus, Virgo and Capricorn
Air: Gemini, Libra and Aquarius
Water: Cancer, Scorpio and Pisces

Other guides are slightly more specific, declaring that we are compatible with star signs within our astrological polarity.

Yin: Taurus, Virgo, Capricorn, Cancer, Scorpio and Pisces
Yang: Aries, Leo, Sagittarius, Gemini, Libra and Aquarius

Doesn't look too good, does it? The most optimistic approach has removed half of the population from your dating pool. It doesn't make any sense. The true picture is far more promising...

One star sign, two very different personalities

Each of us has a unique astrological thumbprint determined by the sun, the moon and the planets. The most important factors being your ascending star (ascendant), the sun (star sign) and the moon (feelings).

Let's make it simple

Imagine your star sign being a melody. All the other aspects (the unique positioning of the moon and the planets) are sound effects, applied by a producer with a mixer.

The combination of rhythm, depth and base creates your unique sound. Another person with the same star sign will get his own sound mix and end up with a different beat.

Your personal melody can create wonderful harmonies with star signs you're not supposed to get on with – and nothing but noise with signs that are meant to be matches. You won't find out until you get to know each other.

Let's get to know your date...

THE MALE

YOUR DATE: SAGITTARIUS
22 November–21 December

The Essence of him

Charming – positive – enthusiastic – frank – outspoken – honest – empathetic – capable of viewing a topic from many angles – restless – attentive – energetic – often ahead of his time – intelligent – kind – disorganized – boyish – adventurous – idealistic – entertaining – in love with love – impulsive – values freedom

...and remember: Although he may seem genuinely interested in you, you'll have to make an effort. He won't settle for a pretty face – he needs a stimulating mind as well.

Blind Date – speedy essentials

Who's waiting for you?

Don't get upset if he doesn't notice you right away. This is a social guy and he's probably talking to the people at the neighbouring table, the waitress or the bartender. He can actually get so carried away that he forgets why he's there in the first place – until you show up, of course. He's an expert when it comes to living for the moment, which makes him easily distracted. This is no fashion-conscious man wearing the latest trends and sporting a sharp haircut. His style is comfortable, relaxed, stylish and classy. However, what really makes you notice him is his attitude: he's alive and engaged.

Emergency fixes for embarrassing pauses

Don't worry! This man will have taken off long before embarrassing pauses become an issue. If he senses that the two of you have very little in common, he will probably make an excuse – or even tell you directly – and take off. However, if you should come across a shy Sagittarius (which is very rare), your best bet is to talk about exotic places you have visited or fun and exciting experiences. Steer clear of anything negative: you want to create a positive atmosphere, not a cloud of doom.

Your place or mine?

Some people might claim that he refuses to grow up, which really isn't true. He grows up but keeps the boy inside – which is reflected in so many areas in his life, as well as his sex life. Sex is fun and exciting, so why not embrace the opportunity when it arises? Although he'd never say so, he firmly believes himself to be a great lover. Whether this is true or not depends very much on his partner's preferences.

Checklist, before you dash out to meet him:

• Wear heels

(hint: He loves women's legs)

• Use a nice, light scent – nothing heavy

(hint: Make him sense you)

• No deep cleavage

(hint: Leave something to his imagination)

• Leave your worries at home

(hint: Keep it positive)

• Bring your appetite

(hint: For food, knowledge and fun

Tip: Greet him with joy and enthusiasm. Be positive around him. If you don't agree with him, offer constructive views and intelligent questions.

CHAPTER 1

PREPARE YOURSELF

Catch his eye, capture his attention
Top 10 attention grabbers

1. A positive and sparkling personality.
2. A feminine outfit which leaves a lot to his imagination.
3. Good legs, preferably with high heels (but classy, not cheap).
4. Unusual ideas and interesting comments.
5. Playfulness and being a slight tease.
6. Not being afraid to stand out in a crowd, in a positive way.
7. Sending hints, without being obvious about the intention.
8. Asking interesting questions.
9. Coming up with spontaneous suggestions.
10. Being adventurous and loving trying new things.

The SHE. The woman!

A good-looking woman can make him look twice, but it takes more to capture his interest. He must feel he's on the same wavelength as her – otherwise there's no point. She must be "real" and convey a natural beauty. She must be eloquent, sparkling and positive with a sharp mind. He doesn't mind if she sticks out in the crowd – this only makes her exciting! Shy and timid women are not his obvious choice, but neither are aggressive ones. The woman of his dreams must be able to handle his ironic sense of humour, be outgoing, independent, feminine, optimistic, spontaneous and adventurous. In other words, she must be his playmate in the playground of life.

The Essence of her

Feminine but strong – impulsive – attentive to his needs – positive outlook on life – creative – supportive of his ideas – independent, but still a solid rock in his life – has an independent mind – not afraid of standing on her own feet – takes care of herself and her body – has sunshine in her eyes – sensual and playful – a good sense of humour – doesn't take herself too seriously – adventurous – loves to travel.

Sagittarius arousal meter

From 0 to 100... In 10 minutes. If you manage to hit the right buttons, he'll be ready for you in no time. In other words, never start anything you don't intend to finish!

Remember: Be true to yourself

It doesn't matter if he is the most stunning guy you've ever met – if you don't match, you don't match. You may be able to put on a show for a while to hold his attention, but what's the point? We can't please everybody. We all have different needs, dreams, tastes and preferences. There's no such thing as a one-size-fits-all lover. Be yourself, and be true to who you are – always!

Very important:

Be positive. The Sagittarius male dislikes pessimists and gloomy people. Avoid gossip, bad news and negative stories.

CHAPTER 2

THE FIRST DATE

Getting your foot in the door
The basics

Ease into it. Take the initiative, but be careful. This guy gets all nervous if he suspects someone is trying to tie him down.

Be classy. He appreciates style and good taste, while bad language can turn him off you completely.

...and interesting. When you have managed to capture his eye, make sure to make yourself as interesting as possible. The more of a challenge you are, the more interested he gets. However, don't overdo it – never play hard to get!

Spark his curiosity. Tell him about something interesting you've experienced and unusual places you've visited.

Listen. Allow him to elaborate on his views and dreams.

Try something new. Suggest having dinner in a lively restaurant, and introduce him to new flavours and exotic dishes. Suggest taking a day off and take off somewhere.

Positive vibes. He wants a woman to bring out the sunshine and someone who will support his plans and ideas.

Whatever you do...

• **DON'T** disclose too much too soon; leave him guessing.

• **DON'T** make him feel cornered.

• **DON'T** use foul language.

• **DON'T** fuss about money.

• **DON'T** rely on your looks alone; keep your mind sharp.

Remember, although he may be frank and outspoken, he doesn't handle "the truth" too well.

- **DON'T** leave everything up to him; show some initiative.

- **DON'T** bombard him with negativity and criticize his views.

- **DON'T** whine and complain.

- **DON'T** restrict his freedom.

- **DON'T** tell him how to run his life – or try to run it for him.

Be gentle – this guy is easily hurt and offended.

Signs you're in - or not

This is usually very easy to figure out. This man can't be bothered to spend time with people who don't inspire him – and that applies very much to women as well. If he doesn't like you, you'll know! However, if he's still around, he could be romantically interested, or not... He is a social butterfly and sometimes he includes women he meets in his extensive circle of acquaintances without going further. Women are an important part of his world, not only as romantic and erotic partners but as friends and buddies. Although this guy is impulsive, energetic and usually all over the place, there are signs you may have triggered something within him:

Chances are he will...

- call you, texts you and is generally very assertive
- give you genuine compliments
- pick gifts that mean something to you
- remember little things you've said
- clearly show his admiration for you in public
- be considerate, protective and shows himself as a true gentleman

Not your type? Making an exit

It won't take long to get rid of Mr. Sagittarius. Chances are he'll probably be out of your life before you get a chance to say goodbye. He knows instinctively how people feel – unless he decides to ignore it. This man will not be in a relationship with a woman he's not on a wavelength with, and certainly not a woman who has lost interest in him. Life is an adventure, so why waste it on a love affair which isn't going anywhere? However, if he has fallen for you and lost grip on reality, he may need a slight push to get out of your life.

Foolproof exit measures:

These measures will require you to be firm and stand your ground – and look really bad. Sometimes a firm approach is better than no approach at all – but it will be doing both of you a favour. Make sure you really want to end it before you go ahead...

- Tell him not to stay out late and to call you at a certain time so you can check on him.
- Give him the third degree when he's going out with friends: Who are you seeing? Where are you going? Will there be women there? You never told me about these women before... etc.
- Get on his back for being messy, and keep nagging till he starts cleaning up.
- Cancel a trip he's been looking forward to.
- Criticize him publicly when you're out with friends.
- When you're out, make excuses on his behalf – even when there's no need to.

CHAPTER 3

SEX'N STUFF

Seductive moves:
How to get him in the mood:

He is turned on by the chase. The excitement and uncertainty... not knowing whether he's going to succeed in seducing her or not... make him tremble with erotic passion. A woman who crosses her legs and allows her skirt to slide up a bit can make him start breathing heavily. If the woman caresses her thigh at the same time, Mr. Sagittarius may break out in a sweat.

Preferences and erotic nature

He is turned on by women's legs, especially if she is wearing sexy stockings. Another thing that gives him a great erotic kick is rubbing himself against his partner – or any woman, for that matter... If the two of you are standing in a queue and you suddenly feel your Sagittarius partner pressing his lower body against yours, you may prepare yourself for an erotic treat.

Less is more for this guy. Don't be too obvious about your intentions. If your attitude, and your outfit, is a bit too revealing, you risk turning him off. Anything vulgar is a no-no. If you manage to take it slow and use your body language in a subtle way, it won't take long before he'll be passionate about getting closer to you.

Hitting the right buttons

Although every sign has areas on the body that are more sensitive than others, individual sensitivity may vary quite a bit. Don't go body-blind. Honing in on these erogenous zones and forgetting the rest of him is not a good idea. Use these areas to create sparks while turning him on, and as a passion-booster when things get heated. Watch his body language – including the most obvious of signs. Open your mind to the sensuality of touch and taste.

Key areas
Hips and thighs

Get it on
If you want to bring out the erotic sparkle in his eyes, focus your attention on the area covering hips and thighs. There are numerous ways of arousing this guy. For instance, if the two of you are out dancing, make sure your hands touch his hips all through the slow-dance. If the dance is really slow, press your thighs against his and just watch how he brightens up.

Arouse him
In private, suggest giving him a nice oil-massage – with a focus on hips and thighs, of course. Although your touch may be gentle, chances are the massage will be far from relaxing for Mr. Sagittarius. Your partner will gradually get pretty hot inside, and it won't take long before your innocent massage has developed into a more erotic activity... If you really want him to go crazy with passion, use your tongue on his upper and inner thigh area.

Surprise him

Take the initiative when you're out in public. Do something unexpected, but only for a brief moment, like accidentally brushing your hand over his more sensitive parts, making him wonder whether you did it on purpose – or not... He loves women who manage to create excitement and suspense.

Spice it up

Roleplaying might sound a bit boring – but not so with this guy! Take on a "hello, stranger!" attitude, without telling him what you're up to ... Notice how he starts playing along. Be a little sassy about it.

Remember: When he's in the mood, he's *not* in the mood for waiting. A partner who insists on doing the laundry first, turns him off.

His expectations

Softness and sensuality. Femininity is the essence. Aggressiveness turns him off. Sexy underwear is a plus, providing it's not tacky. Don't forget the stockings – this guy gets a real kick from women's legs.

Make it sassy. He loves variation. If you're being too conservative or a creature of habit, you won't ring his bells.

Give and take. Traditional positions are okay, providing he gets to explore the more exotic sides of sex.

Inspire him. He appreciates new impulses and will appreciate input from you. Either tell him about previous experiences, and do a little research.

The perfect balance. He's very flexible, but his partner mustn't be too demanding – that wears him out. However, she mustn't be too passive – that bores him. His ideal encounter is a balanced energy, which demands attention from his partner.

Erotic guidance. An inexperienced woman doesn't need to worry. Mr. Sagittarius doesn't mind leading the way. He may come across as a little blunt and direct at times, but don't get offended. His goal is to please you.

Your sensual preferences
Quiz yourself and find out whether this man is for you.

Where on the scale are you?
1 = Don't agree | 3 = Sure | 5 = Agree!

1. Sex is a journey through erotic adventures. There's always something new to explore.
One a scale for 1 to 5, you are: 1 - 2 - 3- 4 - 5

2. When you're hot, you're hot! Seizing the erotic moment is important.
One a scale for 1 to 5, you are: 1 - 2 - 3- 4 - 5

3. Dragging things out is unnatural. Foreplay and intercourse should develop at their own pace.
One a scale for 1 to 5, you are: 1 - 2 - 3- 4 - 5

4. Exploring each other's bodies is an important part of sex.
One a scale for 1 to 5, you are: 1 - 2 - 3- 4 - 5

Score 15–20: Your sex life will be filled with impulsiveness, fun and desire. Enjoy!
Score 10–14: He will surprise you with energy, creativity and spontaneity. Sex will never be boring with this man.
Score 5–9: You may have mixed feelings about his sudden erotic advances, but he will probably manage to dazzle you...
Score 1–4: Sometimes you wish he could take it a little slow. Tell him, because he is very eager to please you.

CHAPTER 4

GENERAL STUFF

The big picture

Keep in mind that the characteristics of a Sagittarius may vary quite a bit depending on where within the sign he was born, as well as a wide range of additional astrological factors. But for now, let's stick to the basics. Just remember: don't jump to conclusions as soon as you meet him. Give him room to shine. Get to know the man behind the sign.

His personality: Pros and cons

Pros	Cons
• Honest and outspoken	• Insensitive
• Has boyish charm	• Childish
• Positive and energetic	• Sulks if he doesn't get his way
• Kind	• Weary of romantic commitment
• Intelligent	• Absentminded
• Is an attentive lover	• Ignores problems
• Is present in the moment	• Shuns routines
• Optimistic	• Postpones boring tasks
• Lives by his own rules	• Is a sore loser
• Eloquent	• Sarcastic
• Loves pondering about issues	• Arrogant
• Knowledgeable	• Restless and impatient
• Entertaining	• Blunt
• Social and open-minded	• Provoking

Tip: How to show romantic interest

With attentiveness, enthusiasm, support and joy. He loves being surrounded by positive energy. Show admiration for him as a man as well, and he will be convinced that you like him – a lot.

Romantic Vibes

Mr Sagittarius:
The adventurous and protective partner

The essence

Embracing life. He doesn't spend every minute on the couch with his woman. Sometimes it can even be a little difficult to get him to yourself. He's always got something going on. A new idea, interesting people to see, friends to keep up with...

The true romantic. No matter how many failed relationships he has left behind, he firmly believes in 'The One', a feeling he stays with him every time he enters a relationship. "This is it, this is the woman!" If she turns out to be nothing more than a faded fantasy, he'll take off and start searching for his romantic dream elsewhere.

Freedom bonds. If his partner is just as alive and enthusiastic as him, he will carry her through life and be incredibly attentive, kind, generous and a perfect gentleman. However, if she turns out to be possessive, she better prepare herself for sarcasm and sharp remarks.

Genuine feelings. The essence of his romantic side is truthfulness. If he feels that the woman is worthy of his love, he will strive hard to make her happy, protect her, surprise her and treat her very much like a queen.

Tip: How to show erotic interest

A gentle touch on his arm, a seductive glance and a smile are usually all it takes. He's got a sixth sense when it comes to these things. Don't come on too strong, that will put him off.

Erotic Vibrations

Mr Sagittarius:
The playful and energetic lover

The essence

Erotic explorer. This is not a fiercely intense lover. He loves the quiet beauty of sex and enjoys exploring his partner's body. However, this doesn't mean that he goes on forever. He's quite impatient and eager to move on from one stage to the next.

Inspiration and creativity. Variation is important to him. Don't worry about showing off previous experience; he'd like that – providing you don't start talking about previous lovers.

A lover and a chaser. Very few men born under the sign of Sagittarius suffer from lack of sexual experience. However, he doesn't chase women for the sake of it. He's simply in love with love and will pursue it whenever he can. This may result in quite a few erotic relationships.

Persuasive. If you feel reluctant about having sex, you won't remain reluctant for long. This guy has persuasive powers bordering on the occult! He can probably talk you into doing things you previously regarded as way out of line – and chances are that you will enjoy it very much as well!

Magic hands. He has wonderful hands and knows exactly how to stimulate his partner. A sensual massage will never feel the same after having experienced Mr. Sagittarius. He can drive a woman nuts by simply using his fingertips...

CHAPTER 5

COMPATIBILITY QUIZ

———————————

Are you banging your head against the wall, or does he unleash your positive potential? Do you provoke him or bring out the best in him? Does he make you throw your arms up in exasperation, or do you feel inspired and complete in his company? Are the two of you headed towards doom or dream? Take the test to find out.

Question 1.
Do you enjoy an intense partner?

A. Sure. Sex without passion is a waste of time.
B. Not necessarily. Emotional closeness is just as important.
C. No, I don't like sweaty sex marathons! I prefer a gentle and playful approach.

Question 2.
Do you find it easy to express joy as well as giving people compliments?

A. Depends on my mood, but I'm usually pretty positive.
B. Sure! If you feel good – share it!
C. I'm no "blah-blah-space-cadet." A healthy dose of realism prevents the world from falling apart.

(cont.)

Question 3.
New ideas, impulsiveness, enthusiasm ... How do these fit into your world?

A. Very important. They're forces that drive us. I love being surrounded by enthusiastic people.
B. Sure, they're important – but it's equally important to keep your feet on the ground.
C. I wish I could be a little more enthusiastic, it's just a little difficult at times.

Question 4.
Do you enjoy your own company?

A. Not really. I tend to get bored easily. I need a guy around to keep me company.
B. Yes, I don't mind doing things on my own. Besides, enjoying my own company doesn't mean being on my own.
C. Yes, personal space is important – but if I'm in a relationship, I'd like my guy to be present.

Question 5.
Are you easily freaked out when stressed?

A. That depends on the situation. If I can't do anything about it, there's no point freaking out.
B. Yes. I hate being stressed; that's why I always make plans.
C. No problem. I'm laid back about most things. A little too much at times.

Question 6.
Does a frank and outspoken guy appeal to you?

A. I prefer a guy who thinks before he speaks. Diplomacy makes the world go around.
B. Absolutely! A guy like that will never leave me wondering about his true feelings.
C. Honesty is important, but honesty can hurt. It depends on his attitude.

Question 7.
Are you a slow mover or do you regard yourself as energetic and impatient?

A. There's nothing wrong with taking your time. It's better to do things thoroughly than making a bummer later.
B. I'm impatient by nature! What's the point of hanging around if something needs to be done or checked out?
C. A little bit of both, really. It's ok to have your head in the clouds, providing your feet touch the ground.

Question 8.
Do you enjoy traveling?

A. Yes, and it doesn't have to be far. I can get a kick from a weekend trip or even exploring a new neighbourhood in my own city.
B. Not really. People who need to experience something new 24/7 wear me out.
C. Yes, but not just for the sake of it – there must be some kind of plan or idea behind it.

Question 9.
What do you prefer? Playfulness and boyish charm or strength and masculinity?

A. I must admit, I've got a weakness for strong alpha-male types.
B. I love boyish charm. Life never gets boring with a guy like that.
C. A little bit of both, actually.

Question 10.
Do you enjoy making suggestions while having sex?

A. Sex is about communication – and there are lots of different ways to communicate.
B. No, I just do what feels right. And besides, I'm a little shy when it comes to talking about my preferences in bed.
C. Absolutely. This can open the door to new and amazing sensations!

SCORE	A	B	C
Question 1	1	5	10
Question 2	5	10	1
Question 3	10	5	1
Question 4	1	5	10
Question 5	5	1	10
Question 6	1	10	5
Question 7	1	10	5
Question 8	10	1	5
Question 9	1	10	5
Question 10	5	1	10

75 – 100

Don't be surprised if you discover he's not the man you fell in love with – but someone who's turned into someone who is so much better. You ponder about how this is possible, but most things are possible when it comes to this man. He makes you feel loved, free and liberated – a unique combination. He enriches your life in so many ways and stimulates your mind. He makes you view life from angles you probably didn't know existed. The two of you complement each other perfectly and turn life into an adventure. Enjoy!

51 – 74

Having Mr. Sagittarius around is like having an endless supply of adventures brought into your life. No days are the same. He'll surprise you with fun suggestions and exciting ideas, and there's always something going on. Sometimes it might get a tad hectic, and you might long for time together – just the two of you. He doesn't mind that at all, providing you don't get stuck in front of the TV all weekend. Come up with a few ideas. How about having fun making a new and exotic dish... or doing some yoga in the bedroom? Flexibility is very important to keep the relationship going, which shouldn't be a problem for the two of you.

26 – 50

He came into your life like a refreshing breeze with scents from a new and exotic world, but chances are that you're beginning to feel the draft and are itching to close the window. Too much excitement, no planning, constant activity... sometimes it feels like having a kid around! That's one of the aspects that makes him exciting, but also a little draining. Thoughtless comments and ignorance are the flipside of his personality. Love conquers all, and if you still feel strongly about him, these are minor obstacles that you can work through. However, turn it around. Do you feel you're able to satisfy his needs or do you expect him to adjust to yours? Think about it... You can still have a good relationship, but that requires a bit of work and commitment from both of you. Are you ready for a challenge?

10 – 25

Do something before it's too late. Make sure to save the friendship even though you're not destined to be romantic partners. If you leave it too long, hoping for a miracle, negative feelings will probably make you feel miserable. We all have different needs. You and Mr. Sagittarius are wired slightly differently and get a kick out of the opposite things – which is hardly the perfect platform to build a relationship. You may have found each other exciting, but in the long run, you'll probably end up draining each other of energy. Hold on to the positive feelings – hold on to the friendship. Your perfect romantic partners are probably waiting elsewhere.

Thoughts...
Just because you disagree on certain topics, doesn't mean you cannot have a great relationship. Sometimes we need a little resistance in order to expand our vision.

THE FEMALE

YOUR DATE: SAGITTARIUS
22 November–21 December

The Essence of her

Sparkling and cheerful – optimistic – direct and outspoken – she'll jump onto the barricades to fight for people she cares about – doesn't take herself too seriously – she doesn't really care about what other people might think – independent – intelligent – determined – open minded – social – unsnobbish, both when it comes to people and possessions

...and remember: She'll be more than happy to give you advice, provided you don't return the next day complaining about the same problem. She will probably wonder why you didn't get the message the first time, and tell you off. She is not insensitive, she just can't stand pessimists.

Blind Date – speedy essentials

Who's waiting for you?

She will greet you with a big smile. Never mind if you're a little late, she's there to have fun and enjoy herself, and there is no room for a muggy attitude. Apart from her beautiful smile, you'll notice how attractive she is. Her hair, regardless of whether it's long or short, will be shiny and healthy. Her outfit is a perfect balance of colours and textures. You can tell she has made an effort. What really captures your attention is her sparkling and positive personality. She seems genuinely thrilled to see you, and she probably is!

Emergency fixes for embarrassing pauses.

When her gaze becomes unfocused and her eyes start wandering around the room, it's a sign that her concentration is slipping, most likely because she's not particularly interested in what you're saying. However, this doesn't mean she's not interested in you. The best way to make her regain her focus is by asking her questions about something she's done or something she's interested in

Your place or mine?

Either. Or some other place if it's more convenient! She is fascinated by men and loves sex. If she's erotically attracted to a man, she sees no reason why she shouldn't have sex with him. But, even though she may show erotic interest in him, she can become disinterested just as quickly. Sparking her interest is the easy part – holding on to it is the real challenge.

Checklist, before you dash out to meet her:

• Have a coffee – be alert!
(hint: Show off your sharp mind.)
 Have a fun suggestion for you to do
(hint: Surprise her)
• Have some good (positive!) stories
(hint: Entertain her)
• Make good puns and wordplay
(hint: Be humorous – and smart)
• Wear attire that emphasises your body – the good parts
(hint: Don't overdo it)

Tip: She can be a tease. Playing hard to get, or indicating that she's more interested than she really is, is her way to check out a guy before making her mind up about an erotic fling.

CHAPTER 1

PREPARE YOURSELF

Catch her eye, capture her attention
Top 10 attention grabbers

1. An unusual invitation, like a Japanese evening at your place, etc.
2. Flattery, but not in an obvious way. Be smart about it.
3. A positive attitude towards life in general. No complaints.
4. Tell her about interesting things you have done or seen.
5. Be charming, forthcoming and a little cool.
6. Being inclusive and striking up friendly conversations with people around you.
7. Suggest trying some new and interesting food.
8. Not taking yourself too seriously.
9. Slight erotic hints with a humorous edge.
10. Not being afraid to display relaxed masculinity.

The HE. The man!

He must be confident and able to handle a free-spirited woman without displaying any trace of jealousy or possessiveness. He must be strong and independent, attentive, inspiring and caring. Having an excellent sense of humour goes without saying, but he needs to be smart and intelligent too. She needs someone who can inspire and stimulate her. He really needs to be on his toes... or she'll be off as soon as it gets boring.

The Essence of him

Enthusiastic with a positive outlook on life – intelligent and with his head in the right place – down to earth, but adventurous – able to discover excitement in everyday activities – sensual and erotic – spontaneous – independent and respectful of her need for freedom – works out and looks after his body – if not successful, at least has a vision of what he would like to do or achieve in life.

Sagittarius arousal meter
From 0 to 100... In 10 minutes – providing you've got her attention. She loves sex and is very impulsive – also when it comes to time and place.

Remember: Be true to yourself

It doesn't matter if she is the most stunning girl you've ever met – if you don't match, you don't match. You may be able to put on a show for a while to hold her attention, but what's the point? We can't please everybody. We all have different needs, dreams, tastes and preferences. There's no such thing as a one-size-fits-all lover. Be yourself, and be true to who you are – always!

Very important: She is a free spirit. Any attempt to tie her down will make her wriggle free and take off. Her love and loyalty thrive with freedom.

CHAPTER 2

THE FIRST DATE

Getting your foot in the door
The basics

No time-wasters, please! The female Sagittarius has a great appetite for men, but she will never waste time on a bore!

Jump in. She doesn't mind taking chances, and that includes her love life as well. She won't analyze a guy for ages. If she has fallen for a particular side to his personality, she will take a chance on him.

A bit of action. She loves fun and excitement. Too many evenings at home will freak her out.

Sharp and smart. Let her know you have an alert mind.

Be attentive. Listen to all the things she tells you (which will be an awful lot...) and give her your opinion.

Humour is the key. The female Sagittarius hates pessimistic guys, so take your problems and get gloomy somewhere else.

Be enthusiastic, and she will soon get enthusiastic about you.

Whatever you do...

• **DON'T** be jealous and possessive.

• **DON'T** be envious and criticize successful people.

• **DON'T** be easily offended.

• **DON'T** suggest traditional date things, unless with a twist.

• **DON'T** be pessimistic about the future.

Remember, although you like her, keep her guessing a little. She enjoys a challenge. However, don't push it too far. If you keep her waiting,

- **DON'T** tease her with old-fashioned gender roles. She

doesn't find that funny!

- **DON'T** plan the evening down to the last detail.

- **DON'T** be too physical, putting your arm around her, etc.

- **DON'T** tell her lame jokes.

- **DON'T** try to impress her with white lies.

she will simply move on to the next interesting guy in her life.

Signs you're in - or not

Even though she shows interest in you, never take anything for granted. If she's not 100% sure about you, she will play it safe and keep a friendly distance. However, she will sometimes do the same when she is interested... Hello, confusion! If you have managed to spin her head around, she will probably take the initiative to do something. She'd rather make a move than risk some other woman stealing you away. She seldom relies on suggestive outfits and seductive glances. Her approach will always be positive and friendly. Keep a lookout for the following:

Chances are she will...

- approach you directly and ask you out
- take an interest in what you do and who you are
- be extra charming and sparkling around you
- give you direct, sensual hints
- organize a get-together and make sure you're invited
- give you her positive opinions on your work or ideas

Not your type? Making an exit

If you find yourself wanting out of a relationship with a female Sagittarius, you've probably cast a spell on her. This woman will often have left a long time before conflicts reach the surface. She needs positivity and adventure; she needs inspiration, freedom and excitement. Life without impulsiveness and spontaneity drains her. Leaving a lover or a partner is usually no big deal – unless the relationship has taken a more committed turn. She will simply move on to the next romantic adventure in her life.

If she sticks around, and sticks around, and sticks around... you might want to send her a clear message. Make sure to be consistent. If you're not, she might just think you're just having a bad day and give you another chance.

Foolproof exit measures:

You don't really need to be blunt about it: being possessive and restricting her freedom will usually do the trick.

- Tell her you're tired of her being a social butterfly
- Criticize her for being disorganized
- Be pessimistic about everything
- Insist on sex the same way, on the same day
- Make sure to plan everything, even the trip to the supermarket
- Question her positive outlook and offer a more "realistic" view

CHAPTER 3

SEX'N STUFF

Seductive moves:
How to get her in the mood:

She is easily turned on – and off. It doesn't take much to get her in the mood, but the challenge is keeping her there. Her partner needs to be enthusiastic and erotic. If he leans back and expects her to run the show, there will be a no-show from her. She'll be off watching TV or on her way to hang out with her friends.

Preferences and erotic nature

She enjoys teasing her partner, not only during foreplay but also during intercourse. When her partner is about to come, she will probably hold back a little, wait and then move on again. This may seem a little cruel, but the climax will be a firework. Many female Sagittarians are turned on by the idea of having sex outside, in a secluded public place – preferably out in nature. She is no exhibitionist, she simply loves the excitement and the sensation of cool, outside air against her body.

Hitting the right buttons

Although every sign has areas on the body that are more sensitive than others, individual sensitivity may vary quite a bit. Don't go body-blind. Honing in on these erogenous zones and forgetting the rest of her is not a good idea. Use these areas to create sparks while turning her on, and as a passion-booster when things get heated. Watch her body language – including the most obvious of signs. Open your mind to the sensuality of touch and taste.

Key areas
Her hips and thighs

Get it on
The key is not to be too obvious about it. Avoid clumsy fondling under the table while you're having dinner in a restaurant. When you're focusing on her hips and thighs, your touch needs to be gentle and sensual.

Arouse her
If you are in bed together, you will soon discover that gentle bites, passionate kisses and playful flicks with your tongue over the inside of her thighs will make her breathe heavily. But, while it feels nice and arouses her, she doesn't want you to keep at it forever – if you don't move on, she might get bored and the hot feelings will cool down. Make sure to read her signals and her body language.

Surprise her

She has another erogenous zone: her hair. When other women would have gone off to sleep while having their hair stroked and played with, this woman will wake up with an erotic twinkle in her eyes...

Spice it up

If she's not used to watching herself having sex, give it a try. Add a few large mirrors in the bedroom and quite a few candles. Although she will be fascinated by the experience, she's also very vain. Make sure she gets to admire herself in a flattering light.

Remember: She is quite liberal and will get bored if her partner fails to inspire her. Try slight adjustments to the erotic routine, or take the initiative when she least expects it.

Her expectations

Get moving. Forget foreplay that goes on forever. The female Sagittarius is usually eager to move on to the real thing!

Add spice. Sex with her is not a one-minute stunt. Far from it. She enjoys intercourse very much and is eager to try out different variations.

Be creative. She is playful in bed and expects her partner to be likewise. Creativity is a great plus. New ideas will always be appreciated and eagerly tried out – providing they are not vulgar!

Well, why not…? She has a strong liberal streak, and with the right encouragement, she may consider exploring some of your erotic fantasies.

Afterplay. Never turn your back on her and go to sleep. She appreciates a little chat afterwards, maybe with a glass of wine, to share feelings – an extended version of "it was good for me, was it good for you'?" Maybe not all that romantic, but very nice and quite informative.

Your sensual preferences
Quiz yourself and find out whether this woman is for you.

Where on the scale are you?
1 = Don't agree | 3 = Sure | 5 = Agree!

1. Too much foreplay takes the passion out of sex.
One a scale for 1 to 5, you are: 1 - 2 - 3- 4 - 5

2. Sex without creativity will get very boring in the long run.
One a scale for 1 to 5, you are: 1 - 2 - 3- 4 - 5

3. Closeness during sex tends to feel a little claustrophobic.
One a scale for 1 to 5, you are: 1 - 2 - 3- 4 - 5

4. Impulsiveness is important, as well as being open to having sex in different places.
One a scale for 1 to 5, you are: 1 - 2 - 3- 4 - 5

Score.
15 - 20: Wow. Erotic fireworks will be crackling!
10 - 14: This may be a little more adventurous than what you're used to. Open your mind and expand your erotic horizons. You'll enjoy it.
05 - 09: If you feel she's moving a little too fast, don't tell her to pace herself. Suggest trying something different, something slower, and make it sound like an adventure.
01 - 04: This may be an adventure or it could be a complete miss. You will either inspire each other or turn each other off.

CHAPTER 4

GENERAL STUFF

_____

The big picture

Keep in mind that the characteristics of a Sagittarius may vary quite a bit depending on where within the sign she was born, as well as a wide range of additional astrological factors. But for now, let's stick to the basics. Just remember: don't jump to conclusions as soon as you meet her. Give her room to shine. Get to know the woman behind the sign.

Her personality: Pros and cons

Pros
- Very optimistic
- Compassionate
- Intelligent
- Independent
- Clear and alert-minded
- Problem solver
- Outspoken
- Creative
- Charming
- Attractive
- Original
- Choosy

Cons
- Fear of failure
- Sore loser
- Absentminded
- Restless and impatient
- Loses interest quickly
- Changes sex partners often
- Wary of romantic commitment
- Blunt and insensitive
- Sarcastic
- Hurtfully honest
- Arrogant
- Vain

Tip: How to show romantic interest

Surprise her with an invitation or arrange something she'll truly appreciate. Even though it may involve other people, the fact that you made an effort will make her see you in a very positive light.

Romantic Vibes

Miss Sagittarius:
The enthusiastic and optimistic partner

The essence

Never take anything for granted. You may be able to spark her interest, but she won't hang around if there's no point spending time on you. A cheerful goodbye, and she'll be off to her next romantic encounter. If you want to hold on to this woman, you need to live up to her expectations.

Loves men. She often moves from one man to the next, simply because she finds men fascinating. Entering a committed relationship requires a very special man.

What you see is what you get. Some men have probably been either discouraged or surprised by the fact that she won't change. Relationship or not, she remains who she is. No, she won't be unfaithful, but she'll insist on keeping in touch with her friends – male and female.

Freedom. She enjoys pursuing interests on her own and expects her partner to do the same. She loves spending time with her man, but she will never cling to him. A flexible partner will bring out the warmth and love in her.

Celebrate! The female Sagittarius loves fun and entertainment. Grab any opportunity to celebrate and throw parties. Be social, adventurous and fun! A bit hectic? Just go for it: your reward will be a devoted woman.

Tip: How to show erotic interest

Be impulsive about it. Be playful and a little frisky. Suggest an intimate flirt in an unusual place... and get her imagination going. Avoid erotic suggestions when she's busy. Either she won't notice or she'll get annoyed.

Erotic Vibrations

Miss Sagittarius:
The playful and creative lover

The essence

Sassy ideas. She's always on the move, both physically and mentally. Her mind is filled with ideas – erotic ones too!

A little fresh air... If she could, she would probably want to make love outdoors. Although she's no exhibitionist, she can get a kick from knowing that somebody might be watching.

Keep up with her. Don't expect her to be patient and tolerant if you want to drag it out and take your time. If you fail to satisfy her, she might lose her spark.

No distracting emotions. You may get the impression that she is holding back emotionally, which might be true. She is not particularly keen on bringing romantic feelings into her erotic world. She prefers sex to be fun and adventurous, not romantic and soppy. In fact, friendly feelings are far more important to her when having sex than romantic love.

Why be boring? She is adventurous in bed and dislikes erotic routines. Due to her restless personality, she is likely to move on to a new man if her partner gets too boring.

CHAPTER 5

COMPATIBILITY QUIZ

Are you banging your head against the wall, or does she unleash your positive potential? Do you provoke her or bring out the best in her? Is she making you throw your arms into the air in exasperation, or do you feel inspired and complete in her company? Take the test to find out.

Question 1.
Do you regard yourself as impulsive or do you need to plan everything?

A. I prefer to organize my days.
B. It all depends, really. I am impulsive, but certain things must be planned in advance.
C. I'm very impulsive and I embrace life's opportunities whenever I can.

Question 2.
New ideas, impulsiveness, enthusiasm... How do these fit into your erotic world?

A. Very well. I love the excitement!
B. I enjoy variation as erotic spice, but not variation just for the sake of it.
C. Sex to me is intimacy and tenderness, not breath-taking activities.

(cont.)

Question 3.
How do you feel about a woman who always speaks her mind?

A. It's refreshing, but maybe a little annoying at times.
B. I like a woman who's straight with me and gives me her opinions. It creates openness and trust.
C. You can't just blurt something out anytime. Being diplomatic is very important.

Question 4.
The two of you are going to a dinner party and you've just been told that you have to wait half an hour for the taxi to arrive. What do you do when she suggests that you might as well get comfortable...?

A. Smile and start unbuttoning her blouse...
B. Become really stressed, and start putting your coat on.
C. Kiss her and say, "Nice try... better wait till later."

Question 5.
When a woman is sensually teasing you, do you expect her to deliver?

A. Yes, of course. Never start anything you don't intend to finish.
B. Yes, but I need to play an active part too in order to make it happen.
C. Yes and no. Flirting takes on many forms. An innocent flirt doesn't have to be an erotic invitation.

Question 6.
Does a frank and outspoken woman appeal to you?

A. Honesty is important, but honesty also hurts.
B. Yes. This leaves me in no doubt where I stand with her.
C. No! I hate to be told I've made a mistake or I look a mess.

Question 7.
Do you sometimes do crazy things in order to get a new erotic experience?

A. I must admit that I do – life is for living!
B. Never. Sex is not supposed to be some sort of sport.
C. On rare occasions, yes. But only when I'm in the mood or with the right partner.

Question 8.
Are you a slow mover or do you tend to get easily aroused?

A. I'm definitely a slow mover; I prefer long foreplay in order to get really hot.
B. That depends very much on the mood and the shape I'm in.
C. I'm definitely not a slow mover. When I'm hot, I want action – NOW!

Question 9.
Do you mind being chatted up by a woman?

A. Not at all. That's a great compliment. I love assertive women.
B. Yes, I don't like aggressive women.
C. That would depend very much on the woman, and whether I like her or not.

Question 10.
Do you feel happy about other people's success?

A. No. It usually reminds me of my failures and shortcomings.
B. Sometimes; depends on who it is and whether I like the person.
C. Of course. Being happy on behalf of others means I'm happy, right?

SCORE	A	B	C
Question 1	1	5	10
Question 2	10	5	1
Question 3	5	10	1
Question 4	10	1	5
Question 5	10	5	1
Question 6	5	10	1
Question 7	10	1	5
Question 8	1	5	10
Question 9	10	1	5
Question 10	1	5	10

75 – 100

You'll never be bored as long as you stick with your female Sagittarius. Never! It doesn't matter what you do, every day will be filled with some sort of adventure. She doesn't need to fly around the world to experience excitement, she has the unique ability to bring out adventure in everyday activities – and you love it! Impulsiveness is important for both of you, and you cherish the ideas you give each other. You may be quite different, but the difference makes you grow. You know how to handle her restless nature and make her feel safe and happy. She comes to you for sensual inspiration and guidance, and you never disappoint her. This can be a very rewarding relationship.

51 – 74

Smart, intelligent, super positive and enthusiastic, she is a treasure chest of inspiration and wonderful feelings! You have the ability to keep her grounded without making her feel trapped and stressed. She kicks your butt when you're feeling lazy and unmotivated, and you make her take a deep breath from time to time and look around her. There may be a few discussions, but that only keeps the relationship fresh and exciting. You don't have to tag along with her all the time. Grant yourself a time-out once in a while and catch your breath. She may be a little exhausting at times – but boring? Never!

26 – 50

This could be a challenge. It could be a positive one or you could find yourself banging your head against the wall. Whenever you want a quiet and sensual moment with her in bed, she suggests a quick one on the kitchen table. A romantic evening can suddenly turn into a bring-your-own-pizza-and-wine party with her friends. You never really know what's going to happen. Which is what makes her so special – and draining. In order to experience complete happiness, you need to be able to keep up with her. Sure, you might ask her to slow down a bit, and she may even do so for a little while, but it's against her nature and it won't last. Regard her as an opportunity to spice up your life and broaden your horizons. You can either take the chance or let it pass you by

10 – 25

She may have dazzled you with her enthusiasm, optimism and charm some time ago, but how do you feel now? Stressed out? Frustrated? Overlooked? Either she's off with her friends, busy with some new activity, or she hassles you for not being more active. Whenever you want to take it easy, she's got some new idea popping into her mind. It's almost impossible to plan anything: everything from sex to everyday activities happens at the spur of the moment! You never really know what to expect, or when to expect it. She is an amazing woman, but the two of you may find yourselves on different levels. If you manage to open your mind and release a little more energy into your life, you may find her exciting. If that's not your thing, she will probably drain you.

Thoughts...

No matter what you decide to do, make sure to do it for the right reasons. Let your heart guide you, and let your mind adjust the course.

...just a final note:
This book has not been approved by your date and should be treated accordingly. He or she *may* not agree with the content.

www.ingramcontent.com/pod-product-compliance
Lightning Source LLC
Chambersburg PA
CBHW071838020426
42331CB00007B/1784